THE GREAT
HORSE-LESS
CARRIAGE RACE

BY MICHAEL
DOOLING

Holiday House / New York

**Buggyaut,
Duryea Motor Wagon
Company**
(gasoline engine)
Driver: Frank Duryea
Umpire: Arthur W. White

**De La Vergne Benz,
De La Vergne Refrigerating
Machine Company**
(gasoline engine)
Driver: Frederick Haas
Umpire: James F. Bate

**Macy Roger-Benz,
R. H. Macy Company**
(gasoline engine)
Driver: Jerry O'Conner
Umpire: Samuel Rodman

The Great Horse-less Carriage Race was sponsored by *The Chicago Times-Herald.*
The newspaper wanted to prove that the horse-less carriage was a better mode of
transportation than the horse and carriage.

Many people were skeptical of this new and strange machine. They thought
that it was just a fad and motors would never replace the horse.

The race began at 8:55 A.M. and continued over the next eleven hours, covering
fifty-two miles across the city of Chicago. Initially, seventy-nine carriages entered
the race; but because of snow and mechanical problems, only six made it to the
starting line.

Sturges Electric,
Sturges Electric Motor
Company
(electric engine)
Driver: Harold Sturges
Umpire: T. T. Bennett

Electrobat II,
Morris and Salom
(electric engine)
Driver: Henry G. Morris
Umpire: Hiram P. Maxim

Mueller Benz,
H. Mueller
Manufacturing Company
(gasoline engine)
Driver: Oscar Mueller
Umpire: Charles B. King

Each carriage had a driver and an umpire. The umpire's job was to make sure the rules were followed. Two of the carriages were electric and ran on batteries instead of gasoline. The Haas, Mueller, and O'Conner carriages used engines built in Germany by the Benz Company. Only Frank Duryea's carriage was built completely in America. Macy's Department Store sponsored the O'Conner carriage in hopes of selling the vehicle in its store if it won. Each man in the race knew that the winner had a chance of mass-producing and selling his horse-less carriage to the public.

NOVEMBER 28, 1895, was not a good day for a race. It had snowed twelve inches the previous day, leaving drifts of up to two feet deep. Despite the weather, five hand-built horse-less carriages awaited the start of America's first automobile race. An hour later a sixth carriage would join the race.

And then they were off! One by one, at staggered starting times, the carriages putt-putted along, reaching the speed of seven miles per hour. Within miles of the start the snow proved too much for the gears on the De La Vergne carriage and it had to drop out of the race. Soon after that the Electrobat and the Sturges Electric simply ran out of electricity.

That left the race up to just three drivers. In the lead carriage was quiet, determined Frank Duryea. Frank had spent endless hours in his garage working on his horse-less carriage—a machine he liked to call his "buggyaut." Frank had fine-tuned his engine to perfection. He knew every bolt, pin, screw, valve, gasket, and doohickey.

Just a few minutes behind Duryea drove Jerry O'Conner. An excellent driver, Jerry was determined and experienced. He had driven before in races in France.

Oscar Mueller was in third place. Oscar had broken down on the way to the starting line and was an hour late. However, he was still the favorite to win because he had beaten Duryea a month earlier in an exhibition race.

Suddenly, Frank Duryea's carriage skidded into a snowdrift. At seven miles per hour, neither he nor the umpire in his carriage, Mr. White, was hurt; however, the steering lever on the buggyaut had broken.

It was a disaster! It looked as if Frank was out of the race. His only chance of getting back in the race was to fix the lever. But how?

It took some time, but Frank found a blacksmith's shop. Because the rules forbade anyone to help a driver repair his vehicle, Frank had to borrow the blacksmith's tools. As Frank desperately worked, his mind was on O'Conner, who was surely taking the lead. It would be nearly an hour before

At last Frank was back in the race. And two hours later he was still going strong when a man from the side of the road called out that he was only twenty minutes behind O'Conner. Frank figured he must have been driving faster than O'Conner if he had lost an hour at the blacksmith's shop but was now only twenty minutes back.

"Ya, ya, ya, hoo!" shouted Frank through his chattering teeth. Everyone was shouting, "Go! Go! Go!" The buggyaut was gaining fast. As Frank passed by, he tooted his horn, *Bwonk, bwonk!*

Before long Duryea and O'Conner were neck and neck. Both throttles were wide open. *Putt, putt, putt.* Each carriage sped along. The race continued down Chicago Avenue and then around the next bend. . .

the buggyaut pulled ahead!

Not too long after that Jerry O'Conner started having trouble. A horse-drawn sleigh tried to cross the street in front of him and they collided. The accident bent four spokes on his carriage, which left it unable to be steered.

O'Conner noticed that he was right near the Clark Street Trolley. With the aid of a few people from the crowd, he pushed his carriage onto the rails. He figured that if the rails could steer for him, he could get to the next relay station for repairs. "I'm not out of this race yet!" he exclaimed.

By late afternoon Frank Duryea was way ahead, even though he had made a wrong turn and was trying to get back on the course. No one could stop him now—or so he thought.

And then his engine started to smoke. He heard a loud *kerplunk* and then another, and then a *hiss,* and then a *pitouee.* Frank figured it must be the sparking device as his buggyaut rocked and sputtered and coughed.

KERPLUNK, HISS, PITOUEE!

KERPLUNK, HISS, PITOUEE!

KERPLUNK, HISS, PITOUEE!

KERPLUNK, HISS, PITOUEE!

Frantically, Frank ran through the snow-covered streets. He had to find a tinsmith's shop where he could fix his sparking device. There was no time to lose!

Fifty-five minutes later the buggyaut was fixed. Frank was back in the race and back on course. Despite the delay, he still had a slight lead.

O'Conner had fixed his spokes and was also back in the race.

And Oscar Mueller, who had been quietly puffing and chugging along all day, was gaining fast. It was anybody's race to win!

However, as night fell, O'Conner's luck finally ran out. He was cold, tired, and frustrated, and so was his carriage. He had broken down again and his attempts to get his engine going in the cold icy night were hopeless.

Luck was not on the side of Oscar Mueller either. The freezing temperature had taken its toll and he passed out in the carriage. Charles King, his umpire, pushed him to the side and continued driving. Maybe, just maybe, thought King, Duryea is not too far ahead?

Miles ahead, Frank was closing in on the finish line. It was getting dark and he was freezing. There was no sign of Mueller or O'Conner. Only a disaster could stop them now. Frank and Mr. White could barely contain their enthusiasm. "Yahoo!" shouted Frank as the buggyaut disappeared into the snowy night.

At a little past seven o'clock that night Frank Duryea crossed the finish line. A small but jolly crowd gathered around and cheered. He was covered in dirt and totally exhausted. The buggyaut looked tired too—all covered with slush. But Frank Duryea had done it! He had driven fifty-two miles in ten hours and twenty-three minutes, while averaging just seven miles per hour. "Yahoo!" shouted Frank.

With the help of his brother Charles, Frank started America's first automobile company, the Duryea Motor Company, the following year, 1896. They built thirteen identical horse-less carriages by hand and sold them to the public. People were now beginning to see how the horse-less carriage could benefit them. Within three years there were more than two hundred automobile companies. Soon people would be able to live in the country and drive to work in the city. The Great Horse-less Carriage Race marked the beginning of the automobile era and the end of the horse-and-carriage days. These early pioneers revolutionized the way people lived and worked. America would never be the same.

The 1896 Duryea Motor Wagon, the first car sold in America

To Jane,
Rachel, Lisa,
Kevin, and
my mom,
Patricia

AUTHOR'S NOTE

Capturing the spirit of *The Great Horse-less Carriage Race* required an enormous amount of research to depict the carriages, clothing, people, and backgrounds of 1895 Chicago accurately.

I began my research at the Haddon Heights, New Jersey, library, reading history books on the race. Afterwards, I read *The Chicago Times-Herald* newspaper article for November 29, 1895. I contacted The Antique Automobile Club of America, The Horse-less Carriage Society, and many others. I pored over hundreds of photographs. I read many eyewitness accounts of the race, including umpire Arthur W. White's minute-by-minute detailed log that he kept as he sat next to Duryea in the buggyaut. Umpire Charles B. King also wrote an article in a magazine. Frank Duryea even published his own booklet, titled *When Chicago Introduced the Automobile to America.* There was a lot to draw on.

Visually, I wanted the pictures to flow to the right and keep the reader moving. Notice how each "moving" carriage is heading to the right and each carriage stopped or broken down is heading to the left. Also, I begin the story in black and white to transport the reader back to 1895 and to evoke the feeling of an old movie or an old photograph. Gradually I introduce color appropriate for the times. Notice the dog faithfully tagging along. *Maybe he was the first to chase a car?*

Copyright © 2002 by Michael Dooling
All Rights Reserved
Printed in the United States of America
The text typeface is Caslon Antique.
The artwork was created with oil paints on linen.
www.holidayhouse.com
First Edition
Library of Congress Cataloging-in-Publication Data
Dooling, Michael.
The great horse-less carriage race / Michael Dooling.—1st ed.
p. cm.
ISBN 0-8234-1640-2 (hardcover)
1. Duryea, J. Frank (James Frank), 1869–1967—Juvenile literature. 2. Duryea automobile—Juvenile literature.
3. World records—Juvenile literature. 4. Automobile racing—Juvenile literature.
[1. Duryea, J. Frank (James Frank), 1869–1967. 2. Automobiles—History.] I. Title.
TL140.D8 D66 2001 796.72′09′04—dc21 2001016589